KNOW ABOUT MOONS

Mary Gribbin & John Gribbin

 NATIONAL MARITIME MUSEUM

 ROYAL OBSERVATORY GREENWICH

What is a Moon?

A moon is a cold lump of rock going round a **planet** in an orbit. Some moons also have **atmospheres** made of gas. The Earth's moon does not have an atmosphere. Some planets don't have moons, but others have lots.

Once upon a time people joked that the Moon might be made out of cheese. Now we know that it is a ball of rock going round our planet in an **orbit**. Just as the Earth goes round the Sun in an orbit, so the Moon goes round the Earth.

The Moon looks very small in the sky – you can cover it up with your hand. But it only looks small because it is such a long way away. It's like the way a real cow on the other side of a big field doesn't look any bigger than a toy cow you hold in your hand.

The Moon is actually nearly 3,500 km across and a quarter as big as Earth. It is nearly 385,000 km away from us. You could fit more than a hundred moons into the distance between us and our Moon.

How we see the Moon

Unlike **stars**, moons cannot make their own light. Our Moon is only visible because light from the **Sun** bounces off the Moon and back to us, on Earth. So if the Sun wasn't there, we wouldn't be able to see the Moon.

As the Moon orbits around the Earth, it also rotates around its own **axis** at the same rate. This means that it is always the same side of the Moon that points toward us, and we can never see the 'back' of the Moon, or at least not from Earth.

But spaceprobes have been round the Moon and photographed the other side. Here is a picture of the side of the Moon you never see from Earth.

The phases of the Moon

The Moon turns once on its axis every 28.5 days. So each day on the Moon is just over 14 Earth days long, and each night is just over 14 Earth days long. Because we always see the same side of the Moon, sometimes we see it when it is daytime on that side, sometimes when it is night, and sometimes when it is partly lit up and partly dark.

The changing pattern of sunlight on the Moon makes what astronomers call phases. The pattern goes from New Moon to Full Moon and back again. When the sunlit part is getting bigger, the Moon is said to be waxing, and when it is getting smaller, the Moon is said to be waning.

Eight places in the changing pattern are given special names.

New Moon	Waxing Crescent	First Quarter	Waxing Gibbous
	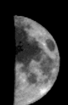		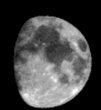

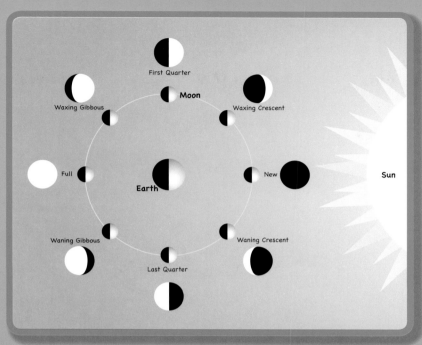

Phases of the Moon as viewed from Earth

People in different countries see the moon in different ways.
Countries near the equator see the crescent moon shaped like a smile.
In the **Southern Hemisphere**, people see the moon 'upside down',
so the side that has been lit by the Sun seems the opposite from
how it is seen in the **Northern Hemisphere**.

Full Moon	Waning Gibbous	Last Quarter	Waning Crescent

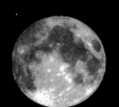
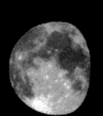
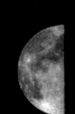

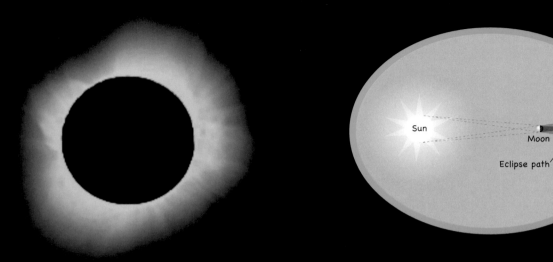

Solar eclipse

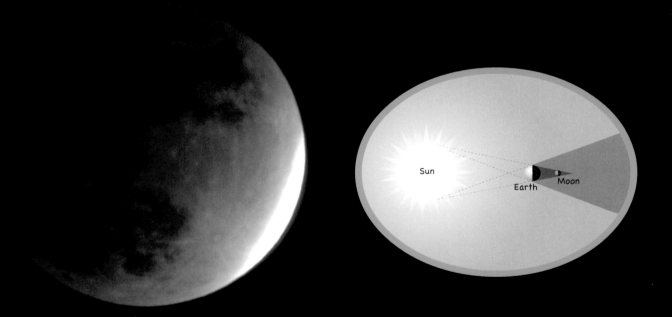

Lunar eclipse

Eclipses

As the Moon goes round the Earth, sometimes it gets in between the Earth and the Sun. When this happens, the Moon makes a shadow on the Earth. Inside the shadow, it gets dark even though it's daytime. But because the Moon is much smaller than the Earth, only a small part of the Earth is in the shadow. This is an **eclipse** of the Sun.

Sometimes, the Moon goes into the shadow of the Earth, on the other side from the Sun. This is an eclipse of the Moon. A **lunar** eclipse can be seen from anywhere on the night side of the Earth.

Solar eclipses happen more often than lunar eclipses. But you have to be in just the right place to see a solar eclipse.

The Sun is roughly 400 times bigger than the Moon, but it is 400 times farther away than the Moon. Because it is 400 times farther away, it looks 400 times smaller than it would if it were next to the Moon. So from Earth, the Sun and Moon look the same size on the sky. During a solar eclipse, the Moon covers the Sun exactly!

Space travel

Apart from the Earth we live on, the Moon is the only place in the Universe that people have visited.

Aeroplanes can only fly in air. They can't fly in space because there is no air between Earth and the Moon. That's why it's called space! But if it was possible for a passenger plane to fly all the way to the Moon (at an average speed of 900 km per hour) it would take 18 days. As well as needing to

take oxygen to breathe, the passengers would need a lot of sandwiches!

Even in a **spaceship, astronauts** took nearly four days to get to the Moon. They had to wear **spacesuits** because there is no air to breathe there. This picture shows an astronaut driving a Moon buggy across the dry, dusty Moon. Nothing lives on the Moon.

The surface of the Moon looks like a desert.

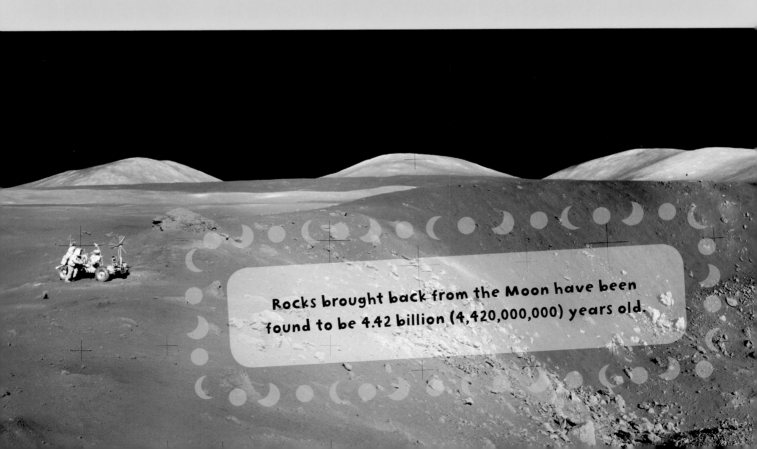

Rocks brought back from the Moon have been found to be 4.42 billion (4,420,000,000) years old.

HERE MAN COMPLETED HIS FIRST
EXPLORATIONS OF THE MOON
DECEMBER 1972, A.D.
MAY THE SPIRIT OF PEACE IN WHICH WE CAME
BE REFLECTED IN THE LIVES OF ALL MANKIND

EUGENE A CERNAN
ASTRONAUT

RONALD E. EVANS
ASTRONAUT

HARRISON H. SCHMITT
ASTRONAUT

RICHARD NIXON
PRESIDENT, UNITED STATES OF AMERICA

Moon landings

So far, only twelve people have actually been to the Moon and walked on it. They were all American men who flew there in spaceships called Apollo.

The first landing was from Apollo 11 on 20 July 1969. All the previous Apollo missions (numbers 1 to 10) had been tests.

There were three astronauts in Apollo 11: Neil Armstrong, Buzz Aldrin and Michael Collins. Collins stayed in the spaceship circling round the Moon while Aldrin and Armstrong went down to the surface. They used a tiny vehicle called the Lunar Module to get down to the Moon and back up to Apollo. Neil Armstrong was the first man to stand on the Moon.

There have been five more successful Moon landings since then. The most recent man to walk on the Moon (so far) was Eugene Cernan, who climbed back into his Lunar Module on 14 December 1972 on the Apollo 17 mission.

The Moon is the farthest anybody has ever been into space. In the future it is possible that men and women, not just astronauts, from all countries, will be able to travel to the Moon.

Gravity

Because the Moon is so much smaller than the Earth, its gravity does not pull as strongly as the **gravity** of the Earth.

Weight measures the strength with which gravity pulls on something. **Mass** measures how much stuff there is in something. Because we live on Earth, we say that on Earth the weight of an object with a mass of 1 kilo is also 1 kilo. But on the Moon, 1 kilo of stuff only weighs one sixth of a kilo! The mass doesn't change, but the weight does.

Astronauts on the Moon only weighed one sixth as much as they did on Earth. But their muscles were still just as strong. So they could lift heavy things and jump high, even wearing heavy spacesuits.

Moons stay in orbit around planets because of the pull of gravity. Just as gravity holds each of us down on the surface of the Earth, so it also reaches all the way through space to hold the Moon, and beyond. Everything has gravity, but bigger things have a stronger gravitational pull. Gravity pulls more strongly on things that are close together, and less strongly when they are far apart.

Tides

Everything that has a mass pulls on everything else that has mass. So as well as the Earth pulling on the Moon, the Moon pulls on the Earth. This helps to hold the Moon in its orbit.

The rise and fall of the water levels in our seas and oceans are caused by the gravity of the Moon pulling on the Earth. This pulls water up into a heap as the Moon passes overhead. There is another heap on the other side of the world, so there are two high tides on Earth each day.

The Sun also pulls on the Earth and makes tides. The Sun is much bigger than the Moon, but it is also a lot farther away, so solar tides are only about half as big as lunar tides.

There are also tides in the solid Earth, as well as in water. The ground beneath your feet actually goes up and down as the Moon passes overhead. But it only goes up and down by about 20 or 30 centimetres, and very slowly, so we do not notice it.

Sometimes the Sun and Moon tides add together and make very high tides, called 'spring' tides (because they spring up very high, they are nothing to do with the season of Spring). At other times the Sun's tide cancels out the Moon's tides a bit and there is a smaller tide. This is called a neap tide.

The Moons of Mars

Lots of planets have moons, but they come in different shapes and sizes.

The planet Mars has two tiny moons which are really just lumps of rock. They are not even round. The moons are called Phobos and Deimos. Pictures of the two moons have been put side by side here. Deimos, on the left, is just 13 km across and Phobos, on the right, is about 22 km across. Deimos takes 30 hours to orbit Mars, whereas Phobos zips round once every 7 hours and 40 minutes. The time it takes to go round the planet depends on how far the moon is from the planet. Phobos is closer to Mars, so it goes round quicker than Deimos.

Although no people have travelled beyond our Moon, unmanned spaceprobes have visited all the planets in our Solar System. They have sent back pictures of the planets and their moons for us to see.

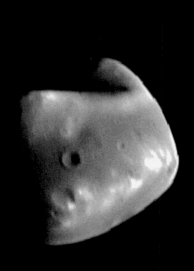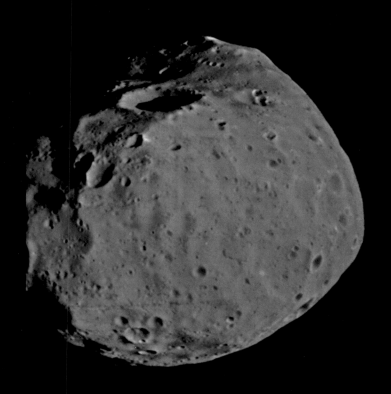

19

Jupiter's Moons

Jupiter has lots of moons, but only eight of them are in proper orbits around the planet. Some of the moons are just little lumps of rock which have been captured by Jupiter from space.

Photos of four of the moons, taken by spaceprobes, have been put together in this picture, next to Jupiter. They were the first moons ever to be discovered going round another planet.

They were spotted by an Italian, **Galileo Galilei**, almost exactly four hundred years ago, using one of the very first telescopes. If you can find a good pair of binoculars or a telescope, you should be able to see Jupiter's moons for yourself.

If a lump of rock orbiting round the Sun goes too close to a planet, the gravity of the planet can capture the rock into an orbit round the planet. It becomes a moon. Because Jupiter is so big, its gravitational pull is very strong and it can hold on to lots of moons at the same time.

Io

Io is covered in volcanoes that spew out sulphur. This makes colourful patterns across its surface. This picture shows Io and some of its volcanoes. **Astronomers** used to think that the moons of Jupiter would all be boring lumps of rock that looked just like our Moon. But when spaceprobes went there they discovered that moons come in many shapes and sizes. This was an amazing discovery.

Europa

Europa is the smallest of the four moons discovered by Galileo. It orbits Jupiter once every three and a half days. It is entirely covered by a layer of ice on top of an ocean of salty water. The streaks you can see on the photo are cracks in the ice. Because there is water on Europa, there might be alien creatures swimming in its sea.

Ganymede

Ganymede is the largest moon in the entire Solar System. It is so big that if it was orbiting round the Sun (instead of Jupiter) it would be called a planet. It is 5,260 km across, and covered in a crust of ice, frozen at about -100°C. The ice is cracked where lumps of rock from space have crashed into Ganymede and made craters, like hitting a glass ball with a hammer.

Callisto

Callisto is very old. It is the oldest 'landscape' in the Solar System. Astronomers can tell it is old because there are so many **craters** on its surface. It has been orbiting around Jupiter for billions of years getting battered by rocks from space. There is neither air nor water on Callisto to erode the craters, and the surface has not been affected by volcanic eruptions.

Because there is no ice and there are no volcanoes on Callisto, it is covered by dust and doesn't reflect much light. It is the darkest of the four moons discovered by Galileo.

Saturn's Moons

The planet Saturn is the second largest planet in our Solar System and has a large family of moons, as well as a beautiful series of rings.

Photos of Saturn and some of its moons have been put together in this picture to make a 'family portrait' (you could never actually see them like this in real life). Their names are quite a tongue twister: Dione, Tethys, Mimas, Enceladus, Rhea, and Titan.

Saturn has 22 proper moons in regular orbits around the planet, and at least another 38 'moons' which are in peculiar orbits and are probably just lumps of rock that have been captured from space by Saturn's great gravity.

Saturn has a strong gravitational pull because it would weigh as much as 95 planets like the Earth.

This small detail shows part of the surface on another of Saturn's moons, Iapetus. It shows the huge range of different crater sizes.

25

Titan

Like the moons of Jupiter, the moons of Saturn come in many different varieties.

Saturn's moon, Titan, is more like a planet than a moon. It is more than 5,000 km across and has a very thick atmosphere, hundreds of kilometres deep. Titan takes nearly 16 days to orbit Saturn. It was discovered in 1655 by the Dutch astronomer Christiaan Huygens.

A spaceprobe, called Huygens in his honour, landed on Titan in 2004. The atmosphere contains lots of **methane** gas, and liquid methane rain falls to the surface where it makes puddles and lakes. It is so cold there (-180°C) that ordinary ice is like pebbles here on Earth. You can see some of them in the smaller picture.

Mimas

Mimas is much smaller than Titan – it is less than 400 km in **diameter**. Mimas takes just under a day to go round Saturn.

There is a huge crater on Mimas, 140 km across, which is one third of the diameter of the moon itself. The crater was made by a large lump of rock smashing into it. If the lump of rock had been going a bit faster it would have smashed Mimas to bits, and the bits would have made another ring around Saturn.

Enceladus

Enceladus has a diameter of only 500 km, and takes 1.3 days to orbit round Saturn.

Enceladus is very bright and shiny because it is covered by ice. In some places there are craters in the ice but in other places the ice is smooth and flat. This is because water has leaked out from beneath the ice and frozen, filling in the craters.

Miranda

Miranda is one of the moons of the planet Uranus. Astronomers have identified 11 moons around Uranus so far, but there are probably more that have not been discovered yet. Miranda is a very strange mixture of ice and rock jumbled up together. Astronomers think that this is because it was smashed apart long ago, and the pieces stuck back together in a different way.

Triton

This is the largest of Neptune's moons and it is called Triton. It is 2,700 km across, and probably used to be a planet in its own right, but got captured by Neptune. Triton orbits Neptune once in just under six days. There is a very thin and very cold atmosphere on Triton. It is even thinner than the air on top of a tall mountain on Earth, and much, much colder.

Charon

Way out on the edge of the Solar System there is an object called Pluto. It used to be called a planet, but it is so small that now astronomers call it a **dwarf planet**. Whatever its name, it has a moon of its own, called Charon. Charon has a diameter of only 1,200 km, roughly half the size of Pluto.

No spaceprobe has visited Pluto and Charon yet, so the best pictures we have are made by computers using telescopes. This picture shows the Earth, our Moon, Pluto and Charon all in their relative size (but not accurately showing the distances between one another).

Glossary

Astronaut
A human being who has travelled in space.

Astronomer
A scientist who studies the Universe of planets, stars and moons.

Atmosphere
The layer of gases around a planet or a moon. Some planets and moons have no atmosphere, some have a thick atmosphere, some have a thin atmosphere. The air we breathe is part of Earth's atmosphere.

Axis
The line round which an object spins. Imagine a huge pencil stuck through the Earth from the North Pole to the South Pole. That is the line of the Earth's axis.

Crater
A hole made in the surface of a moon or a planet when it is hit by a lump of rock from space.

Diameter
The distance across a circle or a sphere (or a moon).

Dwarf planet
A very small planet.

Eclipse
When there are two objects orbiting each other in space and one goes between the other one and the Sun.

Galileo Galilei
Italian astronomer who discovered the moons of Jupiter.

Gravitational pull
The force with which one thing tugs on another thing because of gravity.

Gravity
A force caused by the mass of an object. Gravity pulls things towards one another. The more mass something has, the bigger its gravitational pull.

Lunar
Anything to do with the Moon. A Moon buggy, for example, is also called a Lunar Rover.

Mass
A measurement of the amount of stuff there is in something. A 2 kilo bag of sugar has twice as much sugar as a 1 kilo bag of sugar.

Methane
A gas made of a combination
of carbon and hydrogen.

Moon
With a capital 'M' for
our Moon. With a small 'm',
any object in orbit around a planet.

Nitrogen
A gas. Most of the atmosphere of the
Earth is made of nitrogen.

Northern Hemisphere
The half of the Earth that is north of
the equator.

Orbit
The path followed by a moon going
round a planet, or by a planet going
round the Sun.

Planet
A large object going round the Sun,
or round another star. The Earth we
live on is a planet.

Solar
Anything to do with the Sun.

Solar System
The Sun and all the planets, moons and
other things held in orbit around the
Sun by gravity.

Southern Hemisphere
The half of the Earth that is south
of the equator.

Spaceprobe
Unmanned robot spacecraft sent
to explore moons and planets.

Spaceship
A spacecraft which
carries astronauts.

Spacesuit
An airtight suit that astronauts wear
so that they can breathe when they
are somewhere where there is no air,
like the surface of the Moon.

Star
A huge ball of hot gas, many times
bigger than the Earth. It shines
because it is hot.

Sun
The nearest star to us. The Sun is an
ordinary star and only looks special
because it is so close.

Weight
A measure of the strength with which
gravity pulls on something.

For Ellie

The authors thank the Alfred C. Munger Foundation for support.

Photo credits
Bernd Nies: 3. NASA: ESA: NASA/JPL/Univ Arizona: 26(insert); JPL: 19, 23, 25, 28, 29; JPL/Univ Arizona: 22(top), 26;
JPL/DLR: 20, 22(bottom); JPL/Space Science Institute: 27. Harrison H. Schmidt: 6, 7; Apollo 16 crew: 4; Kennedy Space Centre:
8 (top), 15; Goddard Space Flight Centre: 8 (bottom); Marshall Space Flight Centre: 12; GRIN: 12 (insert). Walter Myers: 30.

A CIP catalogue record for this book is available from the British Library.

First published in the UK in 2009 by the National Maritime Museum, Greenwich, London SE10 9NF
www.nmm.ac.uk/publishing

Text © John and Mary Gribbin

Hardback: 978-1-906367-16-9
Paperback: 978-1-906367-25-1

Printed in China